THE BARLOW IN

1909-200

J. J. Francis

Publication No. 32   September 2009

No 32 The Barlow Institute
J J Francis
Published by Turton Local History Society, September 2009
ISBN 978-1-904974-32-1

CENTENARY OF THE OPENING OF THE BARLOW INSTITUTE

The Barlow Institute and grounds were presented to the village of Edgworth in memory of James and Alice Barlow by their sons and daughters on October 30th, 1909.

A grand opening ceremony was held at the Institute attended by many local people. The opening statement was made by John Robert Barlow on behalf of the family, while the actual opening was performed by the eldest son, Sir Thomas Barlow, Bart KCVO.

On a stone plaque above the main entrance door is carved the inscription:

> `TO THE MEMORY OF JAMES AND ALICE BARLOW,*
> *THIS VILLAGE INSTITUTE IS DEDICATED BY THEIR*
> *CHILDREN FOR THE USE AND ENJOYMENT OF THEIR*
> *NEIGHBOURS. ANNO DOMINI 1909.*

Behind this simple dedication of generosity by the Barlow family lies a long and interesting story stretching from 1821 to the present day.

TURTON LOCAL HISTORY SOCIETY

Turton Local History Society exists to promote an interest in history by discussion, research and record. It is particularly concerned with the history of the old Urban District of Turton, Lancashire and its constituent ancient townships of Bradshaw, Edgworth, Entwistle, Harwood, Longworth, Quarlton and Turton.

This is the thirty second publication by the Society. Previous publications are listed on the inside front cover.

Meetings of the Society are held from September to May inclusive, beginning at 7.30pm on the third Tuesday of each month at the Barlow Institute, Edgworth. Visitors are welcome.

CONTENTS

			Page
CHAPTER 1	Life and Times of James and Alice Barlow		1
CHAPTER 2	The Barlow Family and the Institute		12
CHAPTER 3	The Foundation of the Institute and Grounds		16
CHAPTER 4	The Grand Opening and Early Use		22
CHAPTER 5	Later Developments		33
CHAPTER 6	Into the Second Century		58

ILLUSTRATIONS

	Page		Page
The Barlow Institute 2008	front cover	The Billiards Room	24
The Barlow Institute 1909	i	Early photograph of the Institute	24
Simons Farm, Redisher	2	The Boating Lake	26
Brandwood Fold, Edgworth	2	Institute grounds and Boating Lake	26
Albert Mills: 1887	3	Edgworth cyclists	27
Prospect Mills: 1887	3	Charabanc trip	27
Edgworth Methodist Church: 1828	4	Army camp on Edgworth Meadows	28
Edgworth Methodist Church: 1863	4	Blair's Hospital	28
Greenthorne Farmhouse	5	Gymnastics Club: 1920s	30
Greenthorne House	5	Gymnastics display	30
The old Wheatsheaf Inn	7	The Boating Lake	32
Edgworth Children's Home	7	Institute Annual Meeting: 1927	34
James Barlow	8	Horticultural Society meeting: 1927	34
Greenthorne with library extension	8	Athletic Club meeting: 1927	34
Catalogue cover: 1887	9	Girls' Club: enrolment	34
Greenthorne: sitting room fireplace	9	Institute concert: 1926	35
Dining Room fireplace	10	Institute Cinematograph show: 1928	35
Sir Thomas Barlow	11	Edgworth Operatic Society: 1931	35
Spy cartoon of Sir Thomas Barlow	11	St Aldhelms Players presentation: 1932	35
Miss Annie Barlow c1890	11	Edgworth Tennis Club dance: 1928	36
Miss Annie Barlow c1925	11	T E Clarke Ltd whist drive: 1929	36
Autumn day at Greenthorne	13	Institute Billiards Club: whist drive	36
Walleach Farmhouse	13	Girls Gymnasium: whist drive	36
OS map of 1912	15	Brotherhood lectures: 1927-28	37
William Kingsley of Edgworth	17	Temperance Union talk: 1927	37
The boating lake	17	League of Nations lecture: 1927	37
Open-air swimming pool	19	Winter lecture programme	37
Edgworth Cricket Team c1900	19	National Farmers Union lecture: 1927	38
Decorators and finishers	21	Lancs Agriculture Dept lecture: 1930	38
Opening day souvenir programme	21	Turton UDC demonstration: 1930	38
The Reading Room	23	Lancs CC public health film: 1930	38
The Coffee Room	23	Edgworth & District Operatic Soc	40

ILLUSTRATIONS (continued)

		TLHS: Slide show	51
Annie Barlow & Mahatma Gandhi	41	The Millennium Cross	52
Old Engine Cottage	43	Dedication of the Millennium Cross	52
Evacuees arriving at Turton	43	Millennium Embroidery: 2000	53
Edgworth Cricket Club: 1948	44	Pantomime: 2003	53
Edgworth Cricket Pavilion: 1974	44	Edgworth Bowling Club members	55
Edgworth Bowling Club: 1963	45	Edgworth Cricket Club: new pavilion	55
Enjoying a game of bowls: 1965	45	Horticultural Society Show: 2008	56
Wedding reception: 1962	47	Edgworth Beer Festival: 2008	56
WI: Fifth Anniversary celebration	48	WW I soldiers photographs	57
WI: New Year luncheon	49	Edgworth 'Milk Bar'	52
WI: Craft Group	49	Recreation ground	52
TLHS: Members Evening, 1974	50	Roy Lancaster	inner back cover
TLHS: water wheel	50	James Barlow's badge	inner back cover
TLHS: visit to Greenthorne, 1999	51	1911 plan of the grounds	outer back cover

ACKNOWLEDGEMENTS

I wish to acknowledge with thanks the help given by many local friends and in particular the following:

Neville Coates, Edgworth	Norman Slark, Harwood
Peter Harris, Bradshaw	Dorothy Sutcliffe, Edgworth
Fred Horridge, Harwood	Glenys Syddall, Edgworth
Margaret Higson, Turton	Jean Vickers, Harwood
Stephen Simpson, Edgworth	Mike & Doreen Williams, Edgworth
Angela Thomas, Bolton	John Barlow, Edgworth
Sandra Isherwood, Edgworth	Nick Whittaker, Turton
Local Studies Library, Bolton	Bolton News, Bolton

CHAPTER I   LIFE AND TIMES OF JAMES AND ALICE BARLOW

Thomas Barlow and his wife Mariah (Smith) were a local Tottington family and married at Bury Parish Church on the 9th July, 1820. Thomas was *esteemed as a pious and godly man, strongly attached to Methodism*.

James, the elder son, was born at their home, Simon's Farm, in the Redisher district of Tottington Lower End on the 23rd April, 1821.

Thomas Barlow was a smallholder and handloom weaver. It was in this rural/industrial background that James and his younger brother Thomas were brought up. Unfortunately their mother Mariah died on the 7th May, 1825 leaving the young family distraught.

Thomas and his sons later moved to live at Saltpie, Quarlton for a period, still working at smallholding and handloom weaving. Merchants recalled the young James Barlow carrying his pack of cloth to the Manchester market for sale and these experiences prepared him for a future in textile manufacturing.

In 1845 James Barlow married Alice Barnes of Edgworth and moved to live at Brandwood Fold, Edgworth later having two sons, Thomas and John Robert, and three daughters, Alice, Mariah and Annie. Sadly three other boys died in infancy.

While living at Edgworth, James Barlow started a quilt weaving business in Green Street, Bolton with a partner, which was a financial disaster. After settling his debts, he carried on in the quilting trade at premises in Bullock Street, Bolton, where in 1846 he was amongst the earliest manufacturers to use steam power.

With two Manchester acquaintances he formed the firm of Barlow, Goody and Jones. Moving to larger premises in Higher Bridge Street, Bolton, he employed a hundred hands, as well as two to three hundred handloom weavers working in their homes. The increasing movement towards mechanisation, however, created much opposition from the handloom weavers which led to some looms being smashed and James Barlow receiving several threats. Conditions improved over the succeeding years and industrial relations became better until eventually there was a great mutual respect.

Barlow and Jones Ltd was formed in 1863 after the retirement of Mr Goody – some shares being held by the employees. The company now employed nearly 2000 hands in five large mills, Albert, Prospect (No 1 and No 2), and Cobden in Bolton and Longlands Mill in Bury. In 1877 Barlow and Jones took over the old Stone Mill site in Turton Bottoms and established a spinning mill, Vale Mill, under the name of Edgworth Spinning Co.

Simons Farm, Redisher, the birthplace of James Barlow. This property lies on the southeast corner of the Holcombe Army Range.

Brandwood Fold, Edgworth: the first family home of James Barlow and his wife Alice. Sons Thomas, John Robert and daughter Mariah were born here.

The Albert Mills of Barlow and Jones, Bolton: 1887.

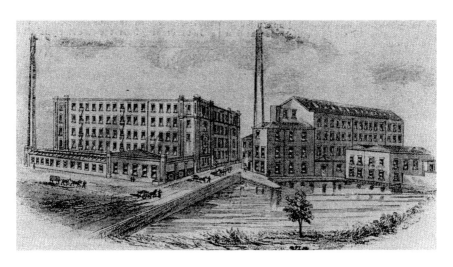

The Prospect Mills of Barlow and Jones, Bolton: 1887.

The original Edgworth Methodist Church in Bolton Road, built 1828 and now converted into apartments.

The 'new' Edgworth Methodist Church of 1863. James Barlow and his family were great benefactors of this, and other nonconformist churches, in the area.

Greenthorne Farmhouse: the farmstead was formed from the enclosed common in 1795.

Greenthorne, the mansion house built by James Barlow overlooking Edgworth.

James' father, Thomas, had died on November 23rd, 1849 leaving his son the legacy of a strong Methodist faith. James, who had attended the Wesleyan Methodist Church from early childhood, soon became a Sunday School Teacher. In Edgworth he attended the Wesleyan Methodist Church almost opposite Brandwood Fold where he lived. In 1845 he became the chairman of their Sunday School committee and later in life a member of the Methodist Conference.

Increasing prosperity in the textile business enabled him to support not only his own church with generous subscriptions, but the Congregational Church at Thomasson Fold and several other local non-conformist churches.

Seeing the misery and poverty caused by excessive drinking, James Barlow strongly supported temperance reform and the formation of the Band of Hope, the Temperance Society and the Sunday Closing Association. He became President of the Temperance League in 1876, advocated the opening of temperance meeting rooms and coffee shops and helped to establish in Bolton the teetotal `Bolton Arms` in Bradshawgate and `Barlow Arms` on Bridge Street.

Wanting to contribute his energies to his home town, James Barlow was elected as a Liberal Councillor in Bolton. He was active in the improvement of sanitary and hygienic conditions with a view to improving general living standards. His interest in education led to him becoming the first President of the Mechanics' Institute and he contributed to the formation of the Bolton Workshops for the Blind. James Barlow was elected Mayor of Bolton for the years 1867 and 1868.

After the 1795 Enclosure of Edgworth Moor, several new farms were formed by amalgamating adjacent awards. One was Greenthorne, named after Greenthorne Clough, a small valley running down to Quarlton Brook at Walleach. Greenthorne continued as a working farm of about 25 acres until 1860 when James Barlow purchased it. Here he built his mansion `Greenthorne`, with a coach-house, stables and an entrance lodge on Broadhead Road. The house was extended in 1884 by the addition of a library. On completion of the mansion, the original farmhouse was renamed `Greenthorne Cottage`. A housekeeper was installed and it was used as an annexe to the 'big house' for the next eighty years or so.

In 1871, James Barlow bought some land that included the Wheatsheaf Inn on Broadhead Road, north of Edgworth Village. The inn had a bad name for cock-fighting, dog-fighting, rat baiting and Sunday drinking. James Barlow closed it and offered the building, 80 acres of land and £5,000 to The Children`s Home. This organisation, recently established in London, gratefully accepted the offer and the opportunity to establish a Children`s Home in a healthy environment on the edge of Crowthorn Moor. This was the start of the Edgworth Children`s Home that over the years grew into a largely self-sufficient establishment.

The old Wheatsheaf Inn, redeveloped as part of the Children's Home.

The Edgworth Children's Home as it had developed c1900.

7

James Barlow in his latter years at Greenthorne.

Greenthorne with the library extension built in 1884.

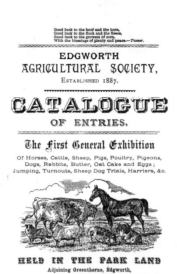

The catalogue cover of the Edgworth Agricultural Society's first General Exhibition held on Greenthorne land in 1887.

Greenthorne: the sitting room fireplace.

Amongst his many responsibities, James Barlow was also the Overseer and Guardian for Edgworth. One of his last acts of local importance was to allow the first Edgworth Agricultural Society Exhibition and Show on May 28th, 1887 to be held on Greenthorne Park land – on condition that no alcoholic drinks were sold!

His industrial responsibilities, along with many other interests and time consuming commitments, caused James Barlow`s health to suffer and he died at Greenthorne on August 16th, 1887. His burial was at Edgworth Wesleyan Methodist Chapel on August 19th.

The local Bradshaw diarist, Samuel Scowcroft, a fellow Wesleyan and Temperance supporter, wrote in his diary: *He was buried at Edgworth Wesleyan Chapel on 19th August. There were about seventy carriages and a few thousand people witnessing the funeral. The road from his house to the Chapel was lined with people who came from far and wide – he was much respected`.*

James Barlow`s widow Alice (née Barnes), who had supported his life`s work, died on September 24th, 1888, soon after losing her husband,. Three days later she was interred next to her husband at the Wesleyan Methodist Church. An imposing tomb with an inscription dedicated to James and Alice is in the graveyard whilst in the chapel is a handsome stained glass window dedicated to Alice Barlow.

James Barlow in his will, made adequate provision for his wife, then left the rest of his estate equally to his children, after adjustments for loans already made to Thomas, John Robert and Mariah.

The Greenthorne dining room fireplace with portrait of James Barlow.

Sir Thomas Barlow, Attendant
Physician to the Royal Family.

'Spy' Cartoon of Sir Thomas Barlow
in 'Vanity Fair'.

Miss Annie Barlow c1890.

Miss Annie Barlow c1925.

CHAPTER 2   THE BARLOW FAMILY AND THE INSTITUTE

James Barlow`s two sons, both born at Brandwood Fold, were highly successful in their chosen fields, both, it is thought, attending Bolton Church Institute (now Canon Slade) before university.

The elder son, Thomas born in 1845, entered the medical profession and practised in London when he acted as Attending Physician to Queen Victoria. He was in attendance at the Queen`s final illness in 1901 and signed the bulletin announcing her death to the public. For services to the Queen he was knighted Sir Thomas Barlow Bart KVCO. He continued to attend the Queen`s successors Edward VII and George V until retirement. Sir Thomas maintained his interest in all things pertaining to Edgworth and, until infirmity prevented him from doing so, travelled to the area to represent the Barlow family on important family occasions.

Sir Thomas Barlow died at his home in Buckinghamshire at the age of 99 years on January 13th, 1945. There is a Civic Trust Plaque on the gable end of Brandwood Fold commemorating his birth place and life.

John Robert Barlow, the younger son, born May 7th, 1852 also received a university education gaining his MA Degree at Trinity College, Dublin. He entered the family firm of Barlow and Jones Ltd at an early age, gradually increasing his responsibilities to relieve the pressures on his father. For the last ten years of his life, James Barlow was ably supported by his son which enabled him to pursue his many interests.

As the only son living at Greenthorne, John Robert, undertook the responsibilities for family affairs after his father`s death in 1887 and continued to live there with his sisters for the rest of his life. In 1912, John Robert engaged the respected landscape architect, Thomas H Mawson, to redesign the gardens, which made Greenthorne one of the most attractive mansions in the district.

Thomas and John maintained the family support of Methodism, by becoming trustees of Edgworth Methodist Church. John continued to support his father`s social, educational and temperance interests but in a more retiring manner. John Robert Barlow died on July 16th, 1923 aged 71 years at Greenthorne, Edgworth and was buried alongside his parents at Edgworth Methodist Church.

The sisters Mariah, Alice and Annie, being typical of a Victorian gentry family, lived in a comfortable but quiet manner, although they entered into the local activities of the village and district. Mariah, born at Brandwood Fold, was the only sister not to remain a spinster and in 1891 married Mr Frank Ainsworth, a Bolton industrialist, and lived at Lostock Dene, Lostock, Bolton.

An autumn day at Greenthorne showing the landscaped terraces and gardens designed by Thomas H Mawson.

Walleach farmhouse: the farm was bought by the Barlow family in the late 1890s to provide a site and grounds for the Institute.

Miss Alice Barlow born at Greenthorne on May 14th, 1861, rather unusually for a Victorian girl, received a good education and obtained an MA at Girton College, Cambridge. However, as befitted the daughter of Victorian gentry, she stayed at home and devoted her life to caring for her brother John and younger sister Annie after their mother's death in 1888. Alice Barlow was a great worker for and benefactor of, the Edgworth Methodist Church and on her death on October 13th, 1919 was interred alongside her parents in the Edgworth Methodist Graveyard.

Miss Annie Elizabeth Finney Barlow, the youngest child of the family was born at Greenthorne on December 21st, 1863. The name `Finney` was apparently given after James Barlow, her father met and was impressed by the famous American Revivalist, Charles G Finney during his visit to Manchester and Bolton in 1860.

Although more well known for her life-long interest in Edgworth village life, Annie was also involved with Bolton affairs, particularly with the Egypt Exploration Fund and Society of which she was a member along with her brother John Robert and sister Alice. Annie was elected Honoury Secretary of the Society in 1887 and served in this capacity until her death in 1941. This Society helped finance excavations in Egypt, the results of which led to the acquisitions of the Egyptian collection of Bolton's Chadwick Museum (later Bolton Museum and Art Gallery). Thomas, John Robert, Alice and Annie all shared this interest in Egyptology and contributed to the Society's funds. In February 1888, Miss Annie visited the `dig` in Egypt with her brother John Robert, travelling by boat, train, horse and donkey - an arduous journey for a young Victorian lady!

It appears from John Robert Barlow's speech at the opening of the Village Institute that the Barlow family, during their parent's life time, had discussed the desirability of having a Village Institute. At that time their own land did not offer a suitable central site in the village nor did it have a flat enough area for playing fields.

After the death of father James Barlow in 1887, towards the end of the nineteenth century, the opportunity arose for the family trust to purchase part of Walleach Farm alongside Bolton Road, an ideal position for everything they needed. The area was to include the proposed Village Institute on Bolton Road surrounded on three sides by playing fields and parkland for the enjoyment of all in the village.

The Barlows wanted the Institute to be free of political and religious controversy, with activities managed by the users and the whole operation to be self financing.

The Barlow family made a condition that the Institute was provided for educational and recreational use, it was not to interfere with Sunday School activities and there should be no betting, gambling or drinking of alcohol.

All the family continued to support the Edgworth Children`s Home and the Edgworth Methodist Church after the death of their parents. Miss Annie was the last of the family to live at Greenthorne where she devoted much of her life to Edgworth and particularly to young people. She was also the last of the family to be directly involved in the management of the Institute

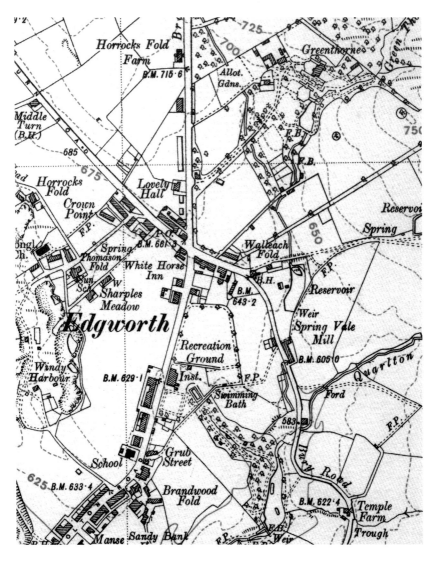

1912 OS map showing Greenthorne, the Barlow Institute and grounds.

CHAPTER 3   THE FORMATION OF THE INSTITUTE BUILDINGS AND GROUNDS

Although the official opening of the Institute and facilities was October 30th, 1909, the actual building and use started several years earlier.

At this point appreciation should be recorded for research on the activities of the Institute by Mr Michael Williams. Mike worked with his wife Doreen as Stewards from June 1976 to February 1996 and his interest led to him recovering the records of the earlier manager, Mr William Kingsley, who worked from the beginning of 1898 until his death in 1934.

Being a local historian, William Kingsley set out to record the ever-changing local scene including the construction of the Institute, the natural history within its grounds and the pattern of village life. William Kingsley was a friend and contemporary of the other local historians of the time, Bannister Grimshaw of Entwistle and Ralph Rooney of Tottington. Being tall and of military bearing, William was often referred to as `Sergeant`.

The Barlow family's aim was to provide an Institute for education and leisure with adjacent grounds that would accommodate a wide range of sports as well as a boating lake and attractive walks.

Although William Kingsley`s diary starts in 1898, local tradition has it that, a year earlier, soil and turf was cleared from the site and supplied to the then new Burnden Park football ground, to re-level the pitch. The first record of wages being paid was in 1898 and included monies to Charles Inkpen, Peter Gilmore, George Duckworth, J J Spencer, and W Kingsley together with Messrs Lever, Connor, Baron, and Appleton, with weekly amounts varying from 10 shillings and 6 pence up to 18 shillings (for William Kingsley). The wages book was countersigned by Miss Annie Barlow for payment by the Barlow Family Trust. From this early date Miss Annie seemed to have acted as the Barlow family representative on all Institute matters. It is also clear that William Kingsley was the manager and very much involved in the design and construction of the various facilities from the start of the site work. The Barlow Family Trust financed all the construction and Miss Annie controlled the management of the work through William Kingsley.

We have no evidence of a professional landscape architect being employed, but Mike Williams did find a sketch of the grounds in William Kingsley`s 1900 diary, suggesting it was in his hands.

General site work progressed over several years from 1898 and included preparations for a quoiting pitch, bowling green, tennis courts, cricket ground and

Mr William Kingsley of Edgworth who managed the formation of the grounds and construction of the Institute's foundations from 1898.

An early photograph of the boating lake showing the old square chimney of Thomasson's Walleach Mill.

swimming bath. The boating lake was formed and by 1900 huts were being built on the islands for ducks. In 1902, the diary notes include `varnishing of the bath` and `re-levelling the cricket pitch`- suggesting that both facilities had been there for a couple of years. From a recorded list of money taken from various activities, it is clear that other sports were also being played from 1901 as follows:

	Bowling Green			Baths			Quoiting	
	£	s	d	£	s	d	s	d
1901	13	17	4	6	6	2	3	7
1902	8	11	4	4	13	4	1	6
1903	12	7	9	4	2	9½	1	0
1904	15	4	3	4	15	4	0	8
1905	13	18	10	6	9	2½	19	7
1906	11	9	1	4	16	2	1	11
1907	14	7	7	1	18	7	1	3

Although there is little evidence, it would appear from posters that the first Edgworth Horticultural Society Annual Show was held in 1903.

It seems quoits was not a popular game in Edgworth but bowling was more so and, with cricket, is still in play today. The 1907 bowling `take` is high, notwithstanding that this year was noted in the diaries as being cold and wet right through summer-so cold that the cricketers were playing in overcoats!

1907 and 1908 saw further landscaping, tree planting (saplings from Greenthorne gardens) and the acquisition of more exotic birds. An exchange was made with Bolton Parks for a pair of black swans for `two of our white ones`: a peacock was also acquired as well as a pair of Egyptian Geese to be established on the lake.

William Kingsley`s great interest in natural history comes out in his many notes on local wildlife. In 1908, he reports the first swallows and a `peggy-whitethroat` on April 29th – nearly three weeks later than in previous years. On April 30th of that year he reports seeing a sandpiper. 1908 also saw the introduction of four hundred brown trout yearlings, three to five inches in length, half of which were put in the lake and half in the Spring Lodge, behind the Rose and Crown, which supplied the water to the Institute Swimming Pool.

Meetings were held in April 1905 to discuss forming a Tennis Club for which the membership fee would be 2s.6d and `bring your own racquets`. A Fishing Club meeting was also held when the matter of leasing Hazelhurst Lodge (belonging to Horrobin Mill) was discussed. 1908 also saw the formation of a Football Club aiming to run two teams in the Bolton and District League in the 1909 season. In

The open-air swimming pool, in use from 1901. The water was piped from a reservoir near Heyhead to the north of the Rose and Crown.

An early Edgworth Recreational Cricket team c1910. The cricket ground was first prepared in 1898 with several re-levellings in subsequent years.

the same year it was reported that the Billiards Club membership totalled 45, each member paying one shilling per year. The Edgworth Recreation Cricket Club had 20 members also paying one shilling each per year. The cricket ground maintenance was supported by the Barlow Trust.

Over the preceding two or three years, the building of the Institute had progressed from the foundations, dug out by William Kingsley`s working party, through to building and completion by the contractors, Hatch Bros of Lancaster. There seems to be no record of the architect who designed the Institute in the ornate style of the Edwardian period. It is constructed in hard red brick with stone dressings, the mullioned windows have leaded lights and the central tower above the main entrance has a castellated parapet. It was a most impressive building and a good centre for the village.

A management committee was formed chaired by Mr W Bailey with James Ashworth as secretary, William Kingsley as treasurer and members R Gardner, S Haydock and J Simmons. The final preparations were made for the official opening with a general tidying, painting and planting up. All the facilities had already been established and were in use both inside the Institute and outside in the playing fields and grounds. All that was necessary now was a grand opening ceremony to be enjoyed by dignitaries and villagers alike.

Members of Billiards Club 1909			Members of Cricket Club 1909
J. P. Kernick	James Stamp	James Whitehead	Tim Ramsbottom
Nathaniel Fish	James Mather	John Hindle	James Brindle
William Hickey	James Morris	C. Fallows	Ralph Entwistle
Thomas Driver	Fred Simpson	William Hough	Harry Harling
Thomas Martin	John Berry	Mathew Kingsley	Hugh Mitton
J. W. M. Bentley	John Hough	William Hampson	Richard Miller
James Martin	Titus Crompton	Richard Greenhalgh	James Forrest
Orrell Whitehead	Herbert Whitehead	Robert Joseph Haslam	William Forrest
James A. Brandwood,	Robert Barlow	J. Mann Greenhalgh	George Mather
Thomas Bentley	Joseph Greenhalgh	William Greenhalgh Sen.	Albert Knowles
Wright Knowles	James Greenhalgh	William Forrest	Robert Harling
Frank Tootel	Ralph Whitaker	Edward Booth	Thomas Hastings
David Alderson	Albert Dunn	William Whitehead	James Duckworth
Albert Miller	Thomas Perry	Jonah Haslam	William Briggs
James Duckworth	Thomas Rothwell	John Morris	Thomas Choriton
			Eli Whitaker
			Albert Crook
			Charles Rogers
			Robert Ashton
			John H. Gardner

At 1 per member the Billiards Club contributed £2-5-0 and the Cricket Club £1-0-0 in 1909.

Decorators and finishers posing on the bowling green outside the completed Institute, ready for the opening.

The cover of the Opening Day Souvenir Programme.

CHAPTER 4   THE GRAND OPENING AND EARLY USE

The opening ceremony was held on the afternoon of Saturday, October 30th, 1909. The Bolton Journal and Guardian reported that `this was an event of great importance to the social, educational and recreational life of Edgworth. The new Village Institute was erected by the sons and daughters of the late James and Alice Barlow in their memory`.

A large number of friends and neighbours assembled by special invitation for the opening ceremony which took place in the lecture hall. The guests included the Barlow family, Col Winder, Councillors R Ashworth, G H Ashworth, R W Kenyon, J Bowling, J Hamer, T Lomax, F Whowell, A W Mayer and many other local dignitaries and industrial associates.

The proceedings opened with a hymn and prayer after which Mr John Robert Barlow representing the family members made an opening statement:

`Mr J R Barlow opened referring to their father being born near here and spending his life in the district up to young manhood, when he left his home in Brandwood Fold to push his fortunes in Manchester and Bolton and how in 1860 he bought Greenthorne Farm and began to build his new home. He was always greatly attached to the country and the people and they had felt they could do nothing more in harmony with his and their mother`s feelings than in trying to improve the surroundings of their neighbours' homes and to give opportunities for healthy and rational enjoyment. Often talking in their home during the lifetime of their parents of the desirability of a village institute, this became possible with their subsequent acquisition of Walleach Farm Estate and there they had carried out the project. The Institute overlooks the recreation ground which the family also presented to the village and forms a fitting completion to that magnificent memorial gift. The Institute contains a spacious lecture hall which would be available for public lectures and concerts, and when not in use, could be converted into a gymnasium. There was a library in which there were some hundreds of readable books and public reading rooms; a coffee room to which anyone may resort, a large committee room for the use of the various sports clubs connecting with the Recreation Ground, and which the donors invite trade and friendly societies to make use of. There were Girls' Rooms for the teaching of cooking and sick nursing, caretaker's quarters and living accommodation for Nurse Turner who is maintained by the Barlows for the good of the village. All the recreational and outside facilities were already being used with the temporary exception of the Billiards Room for which a license is required.`

Mr John Robert Barlow then requested his elder brother, Sir Thomas Barlow, to formally open the Institute and associated facilities.

The Reading Room with its comprehensive collection of books.

The Coffee Room where hot drinks and light snacks could be purchased.

The Billiards Room for use of the various clubs.

Early photograph of the Institute with the Bowling Green in the foreground.

Sir Thomas referred to the characteristics of their late father and mother which had guided the general conception of the memorial scheme and the endeavour to carry out their ideals. The family would not be satisfied until the Institute was managed by Edgworth people for Edgworth people; this was the only truly satisfactory basis on which it could be worked.

On the platform were a number of girls from the Edgworth Homes, in the establishment of which the late Mr James Barlow took such a prominent part.

After the opening, tea was served and the guests entertained with a selection of instrumental and vocal music – details of which were printed in the Souvenir Programme.

Our local Bradshaw diarist, Samuel Scowcroft, recorded the event in a rather blunt manner; `Lizzie and I went to the opening of the Edgworth Institute given by the Barlow family. Sir Thomas Barlow opened the door!`

The activities already established continued. The seventeen Tennis Club members paid 2s.6d and presumably brought their own racquets. William Kingsley continued with his frequent reports. Teenagers Harold Brindle, David Alderman, Edward Ramsbottom, John James Mather and Percy Woods were caught stealing duck eggs from the boating lake islands. The bowling green was cleared of worms, getting a three-quarters full bucket. Annual licenses were granted on February 6th, 1911 for billiards and music. Swans and ducks were sold and exchanged. The grass verge round the cricket field was taken up and replaced with stone.

A crisis was reported in the billiards room when on March 6th 1913, Mr William Holt, the billiards table maker, came to examine the cushions after a complaint that they would not take side. Mr Holt said it was the fault of the players not having put side on. Perhaps to demonstrate that the table was alright, Mr Holt played a game with H Waldron of Bradshaw conceding him 300 in a game of 750 up and won rather easily by 150!.

New gymnasium equipment was delivered in April, 1913 including a stretching ladder and a punch ball.

In March, 1914, the Cricket Club, for the first time, went into the `A` section of the Bolton and District League and the Bowling Club received an invitation to join Bolton Sunday School Social League. In June a meeting was held to form a juvenile Harriers Club and the Swimming Club arranged to use the Children`s Home's baths in bad weather.

Old Russia area in which the Boating Lake was developed.

View of the Institute grounds leading down to the Boating Lake.

Early group of Edgworth cyclists bound on an expedition.

Charabanc trip for an Edgworth group heading for the seaside.

The army encampment on Edgworth Meadows, showing the Barlow Institute and houses on Bolton Road, 1914.

Blair's Convalescent Hospital: used for military casualties during WWI. Many of the inmates visited the Barlow Institute during their convalescence.

By August of 1914 the threat of war and the recruitment campaign led to the cancellation of the proposed local inter-village sports. For the next five years the sports activities of the Institute were severely affected. The War came nearer to Edgworth when the Lancashire Fusiliers camped on the Meadows, opposite the Institute, for training around the area – not knowing at the time but in preparation for the ill fated Gallipoli campaign against the Turks.

By May, 1915, the first meeting of mothers and wives of enlisted men was held at the Institute, one of many to come. The first party of wounded men visited the Institute from Blair's Hospital at Bromley Cross.

Although many recreational activities suffered by having many young men away on duty, those remaining at Edgworth continued to use and enjoy the Institute.

In February, 1915, the new cinematograph arrived and meetings were held with members and a Pathé Film representative. These early machines ran rather hot and needed to be shielded in a metal enclosure with venting to a chimney. The first performance was held in April, 1915 and Mr Kingley reports; *'There is room for improvement and more experience is needed in mending breakages when changing films'*!

Recruitment meetings were held to enlist men for the forces and in December 1915, the total attesting (taking the oath) was 172 over two nights. February 1915 saw a requirement for blacked out windows to avoid attracting the German Zeppelin bombers.

The Turton District Athletic Society Sports Day and other annual events were abandoned for the duration of the war but those at home were able to use facilities like films and concert performances and the library/reading rooms, cricket, tennis and bowls continued although the representative teams were much depleted.

Parties of visitors from Bolton and Salford came to the Edgworth/Turton area to enjoy some open air country life with tea at the Institute. Groups of wounded soldiers came regularly from Blair's Convalescent Hospital at Bromley Cross for much enjoyed visits.

In 1917 with wartime food shortages, local children were encouraged to grow potatoes and other vegetables in small plots round the edge of the cricket ground.

All the village mourned the casualties reported on an almost regular basis and by 1919, after cessation of hostilities, the loss of some thirty-seven men was recorded for Edgworth village and a further twenty seven from Edgworth Children's Home. A terrible loss for such a small community.

The Gymnastics Club of the 1920s.

A display by the Gymnastics Club.

30

William Kingsley's reporting was understandably quiet during the wartime period and it took a few years to settle back into the old village life again, but for many things would never be the same.

On April 19th, 1920, the first Annual Meeting of the Institute Committee was held which established a General Committee of some eighteen local inhabitants and a Finance Committee of eight men and two ladies. Representatives were co-opted from all the user organisations, the Brotherhood and Local Sunday Schools, etc. Auditors were members J A Whitehead and A Duckworth. The accounts showed an annual contribution of £300 from the Executors of J R Barlow Esq Trust Fund. This AGM confirmed the establishment of the ideals set out in the trust, that apart from the annual trust contribution, the Institute should be self financing and governed by the users.

The President for many years was Sir Thomas Barlow, with two Vice-Presidents from the local clergy. William Kingsley was the manager. The stewards during this early period were Mr and Mrs John Hough who were paid £3 per week with free house rent.

Evidence of the post-war recession was first felt in 1921 when a room was allocated for the payment of `unemployment benefits`.

The increasing number of groups visiting the Institute included the Manchester Salvation Army, Bolton Boys' Club and several rambling groups. These groups consisted of up to 100 visitors and Miss Annie Barlow supported the more deserving cases as seen in her notes to William Kingsley - `please arrange teas and I will send down pie, pudding and salad`!

The first electric lights were switched on in early December 1921, but by the following February William Kingsley reported an electricity failure before the cinema show and a crowd of waiting people had to leave disappointed.

The difficult times continued and in May 1923 a special meeting was held to form a `Guild of Help` to raise money to help those hardest hit by the depression. Help was given in the form of food vouchers, which could be exchanged at the village shops and the Co-operative Society stores.

Mr John Robert Barlow died at Greenthorne on July 10th 1923 and after the funeral and probate etc, his executors, including Sir Thomas Barlow, Miss Annie Barlow and Mrs Mariah Ainsworth, the direct descendants of James Barlow, decided that as the Village Institute was well established and operating to the ideals originally set by the Trust, the Institute and lands should be transferred to the control of Turton Urban District Council.

Consequently, on July 19th, 1926 a conveyance was drawn up to transfer to the Turton Urban District Council all the land, 10a, 2r, 26p described on the plan, with buildings, public reading room and club known as the `Edgworth Village Institute`, Bowling Green, Tennis Ground and the Swimming Baths, together with the right to take water from the reservoir near Heyhead, as agreed with Harry Wadhams in a deed of September 30th, 1924 with the following overall covenants:

1   That the premises should not be used other than for a village institute, reading room, club, recreation ground and other similar uses.

2   That the premises should not be used for betting, gambling or drinking alcoholic liquors.

3   That the District Nurse be allowed her room at one shilling pa.

4   That the founders continue to pay £350 pa towards the maintenance of the club and institute.

A later deed of November 10th 1926 was made by the TUDC to enrol the property to the books of the Charity Commissioners.

The Boating Lake within the Institute grounds.

CHAPTER 5   LATER DEVELOPMENTS

The 7th Annual General Meeting of the Institute on January 8th 1927 reported according to the established procedure. The accounts showed details of expenditure and income, with a £300 payment from the executors of the Trust Fund and a modest balance of £21-10s-0d. The notice of the meeting included an interesting list of membership of the various clubs as follows:

Institute Members	48	Cricket Club	96	Athletic Club	20
Brotherhood	25	Tennis Club	43	Girls' Club	50
Operatic Society	85	Library	123	Gymnasium	42

The Bowling Club and Horticultural Society received no mention although it is known they were continuing.

In July of 1927 the 5th Annual Sports were organised by the Edgworth Athletic Club with entries from Bolton United Harriers, Manchester, Bury and Leigh Athletic Clubs. The 1st Prize for the Open Mile Handicap was a Westminster Chime Clock valued at £5, 2nd Prize a cake-stand valued at £2 and 3rd Prize a Pyrex cooking dish valued at £1.

In November 1927 William Kingsley reported on an accident in the Broadhead Quarry where a 40 feet rock fall killed John Hilton (25) of Edgworth, an ex-pupil of the Children's Home. The inquest reported that thawing conditions had caused a fall of rock six feet square by one foot thick, burying John Hilton up to the neck. Death was instantaneous. Another sad incident occurred in December 1927 when William Kingsley`s son Sidney was killed on the level crossing at Turton Station when his towing truck was hit by a train.

For the period of 1925 to 1936 we are fortunate to have access to a scrap book of posters, by kind permission of the Parish Clerk, Mrs Glenys Syddall. Over a decade, these posters advertise concerts, whist drives and dances by the various Institute organisations like the Cricket Club, the Tennis Club, the Brotherhood (a church men`s group), the Athletic Club, the Neighbourhood Guild, the Liberal Association, the Girls' Club, the Amateur Operatic Society, the Gymnasium Club, the T E Clarke Sports Club (Quarlton Vale) and the Girl Guides.

During this same period there were lectures arranged by the Brotherhood who met every Sunday from 3 to 4 o'clock ('Brief, Bright and Brotherly'), the Temperance League and the Workers' Educational Association (WEA) who arranged their first series of lectures during the winter of 1934. The Institute committee also put on a winter programme of talks. The Lancashire Education Association and the NFU arranged special lectures on farming matters like poultry keeping.

Barlow Institute 7th Annual Meeting:
8th January 1927.

Edgworth & District Horticultural Soc
24th Annual Show: 27th August 1927.

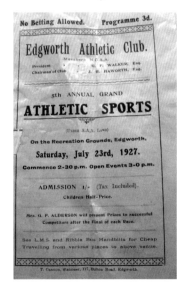

Edgworth Athletic Club 5th Annual
Sports: 23rd July 1927.

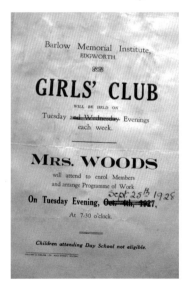

Girls' Club enrolment: 25th September
1928.

Institute Notices 1927-28.

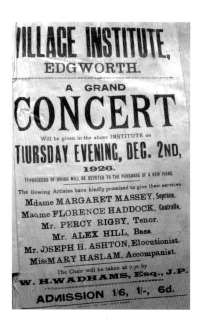

Institute concert: December 1926.

Cinematograph show: Sept 1928.

Edgworth Operatic Society
presentation: March 1931.

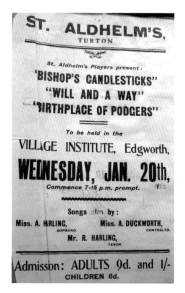

St Aldhelm's Players presentation:
January 1932.

Notices of entertainment at the Barlow Institute: 1926-1932.

Edgworth Tennis Club Grand Dance:
March 1928.

T E Clarke Ltd Sports Club whist
drive & dance: October 1929.

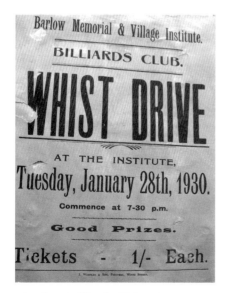

Institute Billiards Club: whist drive
January 1930.

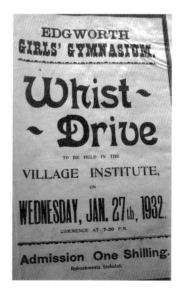

Edgworth Girls Gymnasium whist
drive January 1932.

Barlow Institute whist drives and dances 1928-32.

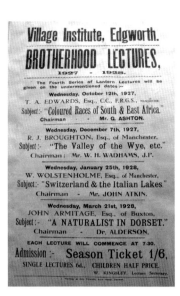

Brotherhood lectures 1927-28.

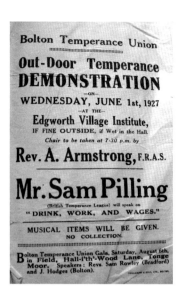

Temperance Union talk June 1927.

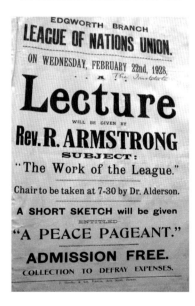

League of Nations Union lecture:
February 1927.

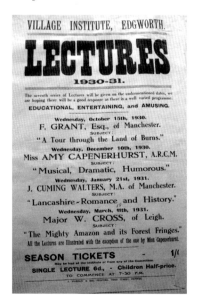

Winter lecture programme 1930-31.

Lecture programmes at the Barlow Institute.

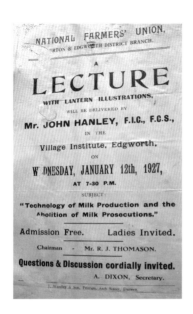

National Farmers' Union lecture: February 1927.

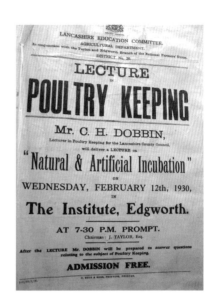

Lancashire County Agricultural Dept lecture: February 1930.

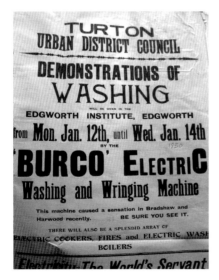

Turton UDC: demonstration January 1930.

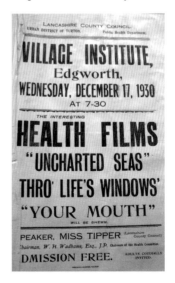

Lancashire County Council: public health film: December 1930.

Special lectures and demonstrations.

The Horticultural Society had held annual floral and vegetable shows since 1903. Displays were put on by the Gymnasium and Girls' Clubs. Special talks were given by local celebrities and in 1934 a lecture on cricket was given by L N Constantine, the West Indian Test cricketer who played for Nelson at the time.

AGMs were held by the various organisations, including the local Nursing Association which had been established in 1928 to finance the village nurse.

Cinematograph shows were put on from 1915, usually with a main feature film followed by a popular serial like `Blake from the Yard`, in the well established pattern of early film shows. The admission prices were reserved seats 9d, others 6d and school children 3d.

Other posters advertised the Edgworth Liberal Association meetings, the Edgworth branch of the League of Nations and covered the General Election campaign from May to July, 1928. The local Liberal candidate for the Darwen Division, which included Edgworth and Entwistle, was Sir Herbert Samuel who gained the seat with 15714 votes, followed by Conservatives 15252 and Labour 7500 – with a 93% poll! The voting station would have been in the Institute.

Even in those difficult times there were money raising functions for the Fleetwood Distress fund in November 1927 and the Gresford Colliery Disaster in North Wales in 1935.

The Edgworth and District Co-operative Society arranged various cooking and household talks as did the TUDC to encourage the use of electric and gas appliances – like the `new` washing machines.

Concerts were regularly given by various groups and each winter the Edgworth Amateur Operatic Society presented an operetta; examples include `Lady Slavey` in 1927, `Falka` in 1928 and the `Rose of Araby` in 1932. Generally four performances were given with prices 2s.4d, 2s.0d and 1s.6d.

Newspaper cuttings, included in the scrapbook, reported on Turton Fair and in 1929 recorded Chapeltown villagers having notices in their windows for `Teas` and `Hot Water` for the expected crowds, but only small knots of people arrived. On the fairground a dozen cattle and half a dozen horses were paraded. The only thing keeping the fair alive were the hurdy gurdies, roundabouts and coconut shies. A report in 1933 quotes – *'the historic event is dying'*!

On August 22nd 1930, the Lancashire County Council agreed a tenancy with the Institute to lease two rooms for five days per week for use by local schools for the instruction of Cooking and Household Management, etc.

1930s productions of the The Edgworth and District Operatic Society.

Miss Annie Barlow walking with Mahatma Gandhi in the grounds of Greenthorne, September 26th 1931. Continuing health problems with rheumatoid arthritis led to Miss Annie wearing a calliper on one leg. A few years later she was confined to a wheelchair.

In 1931, Greenthorne and Edgworth gained celebrity status when Mahatma Gandhi visited Greenthorne. The Joint Committee of Cotton Trade Organisations, including Trade Union representatives, had invited Gandhi to England to meet representatives of the cotton trade who were feeling the effects of increasing competition from India. Although he stayed overnight in Darwen, a meeting was held at Greenthorne. Mr T D Barlow (Miss Annie`s nephew) being Chairman of the Joint Committee, introduced Miss Annie. A well known photograph shows Gandhi and Miss Annie walking in the grounds. Although the visit and programme of meetings were supposed to be `top secret`. a group of villagers congregated at the White Horse crossroads to meet the cavalcade!

In October of 1932, Mr and Mrs John Hough retired as stewards after 21 years service. Mr and Mrs James Whipp of Edgworth were newly appointed.

From William Kingsley`s notes it is apparent that `special` teas were arranged for weddings, anniversaries, birthdays and funerals. A typical tea would cost 2s.8d per head. William still managed overall affairs and official matters such as the license to play billiards and the Performing Rights Society License.

William Kingsley continued to report items of interest, such as the Inquest in 1933 of Levi Entwistle who, after a heart attack, drowned in a field well at Crooked Walls Farm on Blackburn Road. Harry Gardiner, also of Blackburn Road, was killed in 1934 after being trapped in machinery at Know Mill. Harry was a member of the Gymnasium Club and a concert singer. In February 1934 a presentation was made to Wright Knowles, after 50 years service with the Co-operative Society, of an electric reading lamp and a handbag for Mrs Knowles.

William Kingsley, having earlier lost his wife, went to live with his daughter Elizabeth in a property opposite the Old Engine Mill that was later developed into the Bury Road Garage. However, in 1936 William was taken ill with chest pains and died shortly afterwards. He was buried in the Methodist Churchyard on August 26th 1936. Over the years, William had made a most significant contribution to the building and development of the Village Institute and grounds.

The Institute was involved in local arrangements to celebrate the Silver Jubilee of King George V in 1935 and, after his death and the abdication of Edward VIII (ex Prince of Wales), with the Coronation of George VI in 1937.

Village activities continued up to World War II in 1939, after which the Institite became the meeting centre for various wartime organisations like the Air Raid Precaution Wardens and for the distribution of gas masks, etc. The general activities carried on at a lower level owing to the numbers of men and women joining the forces or taking up war work.

The Old Engine Mill Cottage where William Kingsley spent his last few years with his daughter Elizabeth.

Evacuees arriving at the local station in 1939 to be billeted with Edgworth and Turton householders, until their homes were free from the risk of bombing.

Edgworth Cricket Club in action: 1948.

Edgworth Recreation Cricket Club pavilion: 1974.

Edgworth Bowling Club – Turton League champions in 1963.

Enjoying a game of bowls in 1965.

On June 26th 1941, during the early part of the war, Miss Annie Barlow died aged 78 after a lifetimes work for the Village Institute and the general good of Edgworth villagers.

Children of school age were evacuated to Edgworth in 1939/40 to escape the bombing raids on Salford, Manchester and other industrial centres and were taken in by local households until it was safe to return to their homes.

The effects of some random bombs including flying bombs were felt in the area - at Wickenlow and Barons Farms. There were training camps in the surrounding moorland set up for the forces, and a detachment of Americans encamped for a short period on Crowthorn Edge behind the Edgworth Homes. After the end of World War II, the armed forces were demobilised over several years depending on age and service. The casualties reported, although disastrous for the families concerned, were much lower than in the Great War of 1914-18.

The men and women returning, however, had gained a much wider experience of life outside Edgworth which naturally affected their choice of entertainment. Many of the ex-service men and women married partners they had met on their travels and quite often left the village. It seems that the bright lights of Bolton and elsewhere drew the attention of the young people and consequently the Institute activities suffered.

Over this period, the swimming baths had closed along with the quoits and croquet courts. Tennis activities had reduced as had organised football and the annual sports put on by the Athletic Club. The Bowling Club recovered well and had teams in local leagues and competitions. The cricket team had managed to continue through the war in the Bolton and District Cricket Association.

The various displays seem to have ceased, as gradually did the Operatic Society presentations. The Horticultural Society, however, continued their annual shows.

New activities came along like the Edgworth Women's Institute in 1967, starting with eighty-four members under the President Mrs J Barlow.

In order to help boost the use of Institute facilities, the original covenant set by the Barlow Family Trust, that no drinking should be allowed, was waived. A Deed of Modification of a Restrictive Covenant dated July 30th 1971 was drawn up between Basil Stephen Barlow of Dursley Grove, as the son of the longest surviving executor, and the Turton Urban District Council to allow the sale and consumption of wines and beers, etc, on the Institute premises; a step that would not have been entertained during the lifetime of Miss Annie or Sir Thomas Barlow. The original covenant prohibiting gambling remained.

The reception held in the Barlow Institute after the wedding of Jim and Sandra
Isherwood (née Foster) at St Annes, Turton on 22nd September 1962.

Fifth Anniversary celebrations of the Edgworth Women's Institute. President and former Presidents: Amy Wolfenden 1967, Muriel Deal 2007-9, Marjorie Openshaw 1972, Jean Entwistle 1971 (upper). Some WI Members (lower).

The WI New Year Luncheon arranged for the 'Over 80s': 7th Jan 1999 with Brenda Hall, President and George Bentley, Steward.

The WI Craft Group at work, September 1998.

Turton Local History Society: Members Evening, 1974.

The Turton Mill Waterwheel, after recovery and restoration by Turton Local
History Society members; here being set in the wheel pit prepared by Blackburn
Museum alongside Turton Towers stables, 1980.

Turton Local History Society members on a visit to Greenthorne, 1999.

A Turton Local History Society slide show in the Library, 1990.

The Millennium Cross ready for dedication.

Dedication by Revs Daulman and Butterworth with the oldest resident, Mrs Jennie Whittaker and the youngest schoolchild, Clare Conway.

The Millennium Embroidery worked by the WI Craft Group, 2000.

St Annes Theatre Group presentation of 'Jack and the Beanstork' in 2003.

This relaxation on the earlier covenants was of particular importance to the Cricket Club and Bowling Club whose long term plans included the building of new clubhouses.

The Boundaries Commission ruling of 1974 that the northern part of the old TUDC should become part of the Borough of Blackburn with the southern section becoming part of Bolton Metropolitan Borough, affected the Institute in several ways.

The ownership of the Institute buildings and grounds were vested in the newly formed North Turton Parish Council. Bolton withdrew all their support but on the other hand some funding towards running the Institute was received from Blackburn (via a local rate).

Bolton having withdrawn the support for the WEA Local History Classes run by Mrs Marie Mitchell in 1974, class members decided to continue and formed the Turton Local History Society, covering the histories of the old TUDC townships of Edgworth, Quarlton, Turton, Entwistle, Longworth, Harwood and Bradshaw.

The Institute Library continued to be supported by Lancashire County Council until May 1980 when `spending cuts` brought about its closure. It had for some fifteen years been run by volunteer Jim Banks; the thirty odd regular borrowers were undoubtedly aggrieved. The Public Library had been under threat since 1967 but a mobile service now visited Edgworth and District with an official librarian.

The Millennium was celebrated by the erection of a Symbolic Cross near the entrance porch and was dedicated by the Revs John Daulman and John Butterworth, joined by the oldest resident Mrs Jennie Whitaker (age 81), and the youngest schoolchild Clare Conway (age 4).

In Mike Williams' search for records of the past he had found a number of photographs of World War I servicemen. The North Turton Parish Council agreed for the collective grouping of the 144 photographs of servicemen, some killed and wounded, and many others who returned safely home. Mike managed to identify all but one of the photographs.

Mr and Mrs Mike Williams retired from their roles as Stewards in 1998 after 21 years valuable service, to be followed by Mr George Bentley on a non residential basis.

According to William Kingsley`s notes, the Cricket Ground foundation started in 1898/9 with the erection of the pavilion and re-levelling of the pitch in 1901.

Edgworth Bowling Club members relax outside their new pavilion.

Edgworth Cricket Club's new pavilion.

Edgworth Horticultural Society's show in the Institute's main hall: 2008.

The bar at the Edgworth Beer Festival : 2008 (what would James Barlow think).

After a hundred years history it seemed necessary to match the level of other clubs in the Bolton Association and build improved facilities. On November 20th, 2006, the Cricket Club took out a 25 year lease on the pavilion which included use of the ground and enabled them to qualify for a `Sport for England` grant and build a new clubhouse.

The Bowling Club, again with 100 years history behind them (the first game recorded in 1901), wanted an updated clubhouse. Difficulties were met with in getting the necessary planning approval and funding, but in 2005 the Club took out a 25 year lease on the pavilion which included use of the ground, and the new pavilion, with toilets and refreshment facilities, was finally opened.

Councillor Mrs Rigby viewing the collection of World War I soldiers' photographs collected by Mr Mike Williams.

CHAPTER 6   INTO THE SECOND CENTURY

The administration of the Institute and grounds continues to be managed by the Barlow Institute Management Committee. This follows the pattern set in 1920 when the Barlow Estate Executors passed over the responsibility of managing the Institute affairs to the General Committee.

To satisfy current requirements, a new scheme for charity status was registered on September 27th, 2000 to replace the previous registration of July 19th, 1926. This document sets out clearly the objects, administration, form and powers of the Committee and its affairs. A report and accounts are presented to the Annual General Meeting.

The Committee consists of eight appointed members made up of four from the North Turton Parish Council, one from each of the four groups of users, and two elected members. The user groups are made up of similar interest groups.

The current Management Committee consists of:-

Elected Members	Ms Heather Dowle (Chair), Mrs Alyson Whitlock.
Group Members	Mr John Barlow, Mr Andy McIlroy,
	Mrs Gill Pegman, plus one vacancy.
Parish Councillors	Cllr Kath Bullen, Cllr Graeme McIvor
	Cllr Stephen Simpson, Cllr David Wild.
Treasurer	Mr Jack Donnelly
Secretary	Mrs Glenys Syddall

The Management Committee in conjunction with the user organisations are planning various events to mark the Opening Centenary and this booklet is a contribution by the Turton Local History Society.

It is pleasing to report that the current usage of the Barlow Institute and grounds is still thriving in this anniversary year.

The Cricket Club continues to perform well in the Bolton Cricket Association and is now able to equal their fellow Association teams with new pavilion facilities. Similarly the Bowling Club continues to take part in local leagues and competitions and is also able to offer improved pavilion facilities to visiting teams. Both these clubs have passed their `hundred` in terms of their active life.

The other outside facilities continue but in a non-competitive and friendly form. The tennis courts are available to players, as is the adjacent field for football and

The Edgworth 'Milk Bar', a new support group for mums and babies.

The Recreation Ground behind the Institute, for local youngsters. Tennis courts are to the rear: 2008.

rounders. The children`s playground is well equipped and regularly used by families and their younger children. The surrounding parkland includes footpaths where anyone can enjoy a sample of Edgworth countryside.

In the Institute, regular weekly activities are held, including computer classes for both users and beginners. There are weekly meetings for the more mature residents with an Over 60s Club and Luncheon Club run by local volunteers and an Over 50s Exercise Group. For the more energetic there are classes in Yoga and line dancing, while the youngsters have a Mums and Tots Group and a Tea-Time Club.

Local teenagers are encouraged to utilise the Youth Club and have the use of the billiards tables. Those seeking involvement in practical subjects can join the Decoupage Group, the Craft Group who are currently working on a Centenary Tapestry, or the Railway Group. Up to quite recently a group of members put on an ambitious Christmas pantomime for the enjoyment of local families.

A weekly Police Surgery is also held in the Institute to enable residents to discuss the area problems with their local constabulary. The Parish Council Meetings are held once a month which residents may attend as observers.

A special Reading Group is held once a month as are meetings of the Turton Local History Society, the Edgworth and District Women`s Institute and the Edgworth and District Horticultural Society.

All the above organisations welcome new members and details are available at the Institute.

One can see from this brief description of current activities that the Barlow Institute and its grounds are very much alive and well and continue to offer what the original Barlow Trust intended – to provide for both the educational and recreational needs of Edgworth people.